AF597049

Why Men Hit Their Wives

Refuse To Be Abused

CELINA CASE

COPY RIGHT @2022
CELINA CASE
ALL RIGHT RESERVED

CHAPTER FOUR

CHAPTER FIVE

INTRODUCTION

A spouse abuser will in general be loaded up with outrage, hatred, doubt, strain and dread. Frequently the spouse may essentially be dislodging his displeasure about his circumstance or conditions onto his significant other. He is, basically, involving her as a vent for the disappointments of his life. He accepts that house is one spot where he can communicate those sentiments without discipline to himself. For example, outrage with his supervisor couldn't be followed up on without critical conditions. However, over and over again he moves away without punishment when he beats his significant other. She turns into the objective of his retribution, and he gets the fulfillment he is searching for.

The abusive husband often exhibits the following traits

1. He has low confidence.

2. He faults conditions for his concerns and doesn't take care of his activities.

3. He is neurotically envious, and frequently shows a double character.

4. He has extreme pressure responses, during which he utilizes drinking and spouse battering to adapt.

5. He habitually involves sex as a demonstration of hostility to improve his confidence considering winding down virility.

6. The oppressive spouse shows flighty way of behaving, deprecates his accomplice,

seethes with uncontrolled outrage and later frequently requests another opportunity.

7. Harmful spouses are chameleons.

They say they will change and won't hit in the future. They play on their spouses culpability on the off chance that you adored me, you would.

8. Ostensibly, the victimizer might appear to be enchanting, gregarious and, surprisingly, delicate to relatives. However, underneath the surface they hate ladies and accept that a lady's place is in the home and that men reserve the option to control ladies.

9. They frequently saw maltreatment in their home growing up, and often misuse their youngsters too.

10. They separate the family. Separation from loved ones is a vital objective for the abuser since it powers the casualty into all out accommodation. Your family brings a lot of hardship for us.

I don't need you seeing them any longer.

Most ladies languish these assaults over years before they at long last decide to do whatever it may take to hold back from being casualties or further maltreatment. The initial step for a lady to take is to own up to herself that she is being manhandled and that she isn't being dealt with reasonably. She has the option to have a solid sense of security from actual damage, particularly in her own home. Nobody, including a spouse, has the option to hurt another person. Likewise, mishandled ladies need to chip away at their mental self portrait with a confided in guide or minister to foster better sentiments about themselves.

The accompanying perspectives are positive and helpful. God's Statement lets us know we are cherished and esteemed by Him; however, the manhandled spouse frequently trusts lies and is misled by Satan.

Here are a few insights to carry profound recuperating to the battered spouse.

She isn't to be faulted for being beaten and mishandled.

She isn't the reason for another's way of behaving.

She shouldn't like or need the maltreatment.

She doesn't, I rehash, doesn't need to take it.

She is a commendable lady, valuable to God, and should be treated with deference. She has Divine ability to assume responsibility for her life. She can utilize that power and the beauty of God to deal with herself, to conclude what is best for herself as well as her kids, and can make changes in her day to day existence.

She is rarely alone. Jesus vowed not to leave her or neglect her.

Dear spouse, you can ask others for help. The Body of Christ and Christian counselors are prepared to help and support you. Crisis covers for ladies, hotlines, ladies' associations, social help offices, local area emotional wellness habitats and medical clinic trauma centers are protected spots for cover. You have the right to make your own life protected and blissful, and can hold expect what's to come.

For your Creator is your spouse the Ruler All-powerful is His name. The Sacred One of Israel is your Deliverer; He is known as the Divine force of all the earth. Isaiah 54:5.

CHAPTER ONE

Heartbreaking Reasons Why Men Hit The Women They Love

For what reason are most men so aggressive, underhanded, overbearing, inconsiderate, and bossy, For what reason do a few spouses beat their wives like little kids.

What right do you need to beat an individual grown-up and the mother of your kids, for what reason are you so impolite and negligent, why genuinely hurt the lady you once went through restless evenings pondering. What happened to, I will cherish you perpetually, why this abuse, For what reason is she generally melancholic when you are near, why every one of the affronts before the kids, For how long are you wanting to continue to make her exuberantly pleased and mind with agony and second thoughts.

She was blissful before you came into her life thus, I accept she will make it without you. Quit making her your detainee.

Quit torturing her. She may be under your leniency now, however one thing is without a doubt: She can undoubtedly get up on her feet once more.

Let her go on the off chance that you don't need her any longer.

I don't have the foggiest idea why you treat her along these lines, yet you don't believe that she should go.

This is confounding. I want replies. I really want coherent reasons.

I frantically need to know why.

I sympathize with your aggravation and disappointment ladies go through. I'm heartbroken that a few men have not satisfied their call to be the spouses, watchmen, defenders, and clerics of their homes.

I additionally realize that a few ladies have made it challenging for their men to cherish them how they are called to do. In this way, I concur that something is very off-base in the event that I pivot and utilize actual power, misuse, and fail to attempt to have my direction with an individual I once genuinely cherished and yearned to live with. It is to be sure a miserable undertaking.

I don't have your significant other's side of the story, so my recommendation is honestly subject to the reality of your point of view.

Numerous advisors concur that aggressive behavior at home and misuse are utilized for one plan: To acquire and keep up with complete command over the individual being manhandled. An oppressive man will cause dread, culpability, disgrace, actual agony, and terrorizing to wear you out and hold you powerless to resist him. At the point when your man compromises you, genuinely harms you, or damages everyone around you, you really want to find a striking way to safeguard your life and the existences of those you love by detailing such cases.

What Really Makes Some People In Relationships Turn Abusive And Uncaring

In the first place, you really want to figure out what makes your man become oppressive. Is it due to the manner in which you answer him, For instance, certain individuals' oppressive way of behaving is set off by how they feel treated. Now and again, such maltreatment could be kept away from by how issues are drawn closer and taken care of. Besides, you really want to figure out what regularly happens when a maltreatment happens. Most victimizers go on in their propensity since they have acquired the expertise of threatening those they misuse. They feel that they have the right, thus they move about like nothing would contact them. What you ought to never do is to give him the option to manhandle you by staying silent or capitulating to terrorizing.

Why Do Men Hit Women They Supposedly Love

In an effort to understand domestic violence and abusive relationships, batterers and their reasons for their violent behavior toward women.

1. Abusers have a serious need to control the ladies they love.

The greatest confusion about these folks is that they have outrage the executives issues. They don't really.

They don't explode at work or at the driver who cuts into their path. All things being equal, they have a staggering need to control their adored one how she dresses, where she goes, and whom she converses with.

That is the reason, before they really begin utilizing actual savagery to remain in charge, they are frequently continually calling and text informing the object of their warm gestures so they know precisely exact thing she's doing consistently.

2. Abusers frequently do truly cherish the ladies they beat up.

As a matter of fact, they are in many cases fanatically enamored with their sweethearts or spouses, which makes them significantly more desirous and controlling they simply don't have a clue about the legitimate method for communicating it.

3. Abusers commonly fault their lady friends for constraining them to be savage.

A Abusers will tell himself and his better half that she incited the brutality by taking a gander at another person, wearing a skirt that is excessively short, or not tidying up the kitchen quickly enough.

4. Furthermore, ladies normally fault themselves for inciting their beaus.

They get conditioned into accepting that they've accomplished something wrong. It was my problem for driving him to think I was cheating.

5. At the point when Abusers apologize, it's one more type of assuming command.

Men who misuse ladies can be decisively contrite crying, asking for absolution and promising to at absolutely no point ever become rough in the future. Roses and gifts can be ordinary.

6. Folks who misuse are unreliable and have unfortunate motivation control.

It's unusual. They can appear to be totally typical and stable now and again. At work, they can introduce themselves as totally pleasant guys. It's the apprehension about losing their girlfriend or being not able to control her that prompts the extreme explosions of fury and brutality.

7. At the point when folks misuse, they feel qualified for make it happen.

They accept they reserve the privilege to utilize whatever implies important to assume command over the circumstance.

In the event that police show up, they aren't embarrassed about their way of behaving; they feel supported i.e., You merited it you were acting like a skank.

8. If your boyfriend is violent, it's unlikely he will be cured.

Most abusers don't get the treatment they need in order to stop. They don't want help because they believe they are in the right.

Furthermore, the beatings are likely to escalate over time.

Ask for help from your close friends, family or a domestic abuse organization, and make a plan to leave ASAP.

Domestic Violence

What's the difference between normal conflict and domestic violence? Conflict is part of every intimate relationship that's why conflict resolution skills are important. Domestic violence, however, has no place in a healthy relationship, whether the couple is dating, cohabiting, engaged, or married.

What Domestic Violence Mean

Abusive behavior at home is any sort of conduct that a person purposes, or takes steps to use, to control a personal partner.

The two key components are danger and control.

Abusive behavior at home can take different structures:

Actual Savage activities like hitting, beating, pushing, and kicking. As a rule, actual maltreatment turns out to be more successive and serious after some time.

Sexual Incorporates any sexual demonstrations that are constrained on one partner by the other.

Mental Incorporates a large number of ways of behaving, for example, terrorizing, detaching the casualty from loved ones, controlling where the casualty goes, causing the casualty to feel remorseful or insane, and setting nonsensical expectations

Close to home Subverting a singular's confidence, steady analysis, affronts, put-downs, and ridiculing.

Monetary Models incorporate restricting the casualty's admittance to family pay, keeping the casualty from working or constraining the casualty to work, obliterating the casualty's property, and settling on every one of the monetary choices.

All kinds of people can be survivors of homegrown maltreatment. As per the Public Abusive behavior at home Hotline measurements, around 1 of every 4 ladies and 1 out of 7 men beyond 18 years old have been the casualty of actual abusive behavior at home, and practically half of the two genders have encountered some type of homegrown mental animosity.

Characteristics Of Victims

Female, although men can also experience domestic violence

Younger, often in their 20’s and 30’s

More likely to be dating or cohabiting than married

Nearly half live in households with children

Why Do Women Stay

Women frequently stay with their abusers due to fear. They are worried about the possibility that that the victimizer will turn out to be more savage assuming they attempt to leave. Some trepidation that they will lose their youngsters. Many accept that they can't make it all alone.

A few manhandled ladies accept that the maltreatment is their shortcoming. They feel that they can stop the maltreatment on the off chance that they simply act in an unexpected way. Some can't concede that they are mishandled ladies. Others feel constrained to remain in the relationship. They might feel cut off from social help and assets. Mishandled ladies frequently feel that they are distant from everyone else, and have no where to go for help.

Why Do Men Batter

Abusive men come from all walks of life. They might find success in their vocation and regarded in their congregation and local area. Abusive men frequently share a few normal qualities.

They tend to be jealous, possessive and easily angered.

Many abusive men believe that women are inferior.

They accept that men are intended to overwhelm and control ladies. Regularly, harmful men reject that the maltreatment is going on or they limit it. They might fault their partner for the maltreatment, saying, you caused me to do this.

Liquor and medications are frequently connected with aggressive behavior at home yet they don't cause it. A harmful man who beverages or utilizations drugs has two unique issues: substance misuse and brutality. Both should be dealt with.

CHAPTER TWO

What The Church Teaches About Domestic Violence

The U.S. church Bishops have clarified that viciousness against women, inside or outside the house, is rarely legitimate. Brutality in any structure physical, sexual, mental, or verbal is wicked; frequently it is a wrongdoing too.

Where To Find Help

For Abused Persons

Accept that you are in good company. Help is accessible for yourself as well as your children. Talk in confidence to someone you trust: a family member, friend, pastor or family doctor. In the event that you decide to remain in the circumstance, set up a strategy to guarantee your wellbeing. This incorporates concealing a vehicle key, person records, and a few cash in a protected spot and finding some place to go in a crisis.

For Those Who Abuse

Concede that the maltreatment is your concern, not your partner's. Start to accept that you can change your way of behaving assuming you decide to do as such.

Connect for help. Converse with someone you trust who can assist you with assessing what is happening. Contact church Causes or other church or local area organizations for the name of a program for wrongdoers.

Domestic Violence And The Permanence Of Marriage

A few mishandled ladies accept that Church showing on the lastingness of marriage expects them to remain in an oppressive relationship. They might wonder whether or not to look for a division or separation.

They might expect that they can't re-wed in the Church.

In When I Call for Help: A Peaceful Reaction to Abusive behavior at home Against Ladies, the Catholic diocesans stress that no individual is supposed to remain in a harmful marriage. Viciousness and misuse, not separate, separate a marriage.

The victimizer has proactively broken the marriage contract through their harmful way of behaving. Mishandled people who have separated might need to explore the chance of looking for a revocation.

What The Bible Says

Oppressive men might take a text from the Book of scriptures and twist it to help their entitlement to hitter. They frequently use Ephesians 5:22 Spouses ought to be subordinate to their husbands with regards to the Master to legitimize their way of behaving. This entry (v. 21-33), in any case, alludes to the common accommodation of a couple out of affection for Christ.

It implies that spouses ought to cherish their wives as they love their own body, as Christ adores the Congregation.

The Catholic bishops censure the utilization of the bible to help oppressive conduct in any structure. People are made in God's picture. They are to treat each other with poise and regard.

Forgiveness

Men who player likewise refer to the Bible to demand that their casualties excuse them see, for instance, Matthew 6:9-15.

A casualty then feels regretful on the off chance that she can't do as such. Forgiveness, nonetheless, doesn't mean failing to remember the maltreatment or imagining that it didn't work out. Nor is conceivable.

Pardoning isn't consent to rehash the maltreatment. Rather, pardoning implies that the casualty chooses to relinquish the experience, to continue on with life and not to endure maltreatment of any sort once more.

Abusive Personality

Numerous ladies are keen on ways of detecting a likely abuser, particularly whenever they have been engaged with a harmful relationship. Beneath you will find a rundown of ways of behaving found in victimizers; the last four signs recorded are oppressive ways of behaving that

are many times disregarded as the start of actual maltreatment.

In the event that an individual shows a few of different ways of behaving, say three

to more, there is areas of strength for a for actual brutality.

The more signs an individual has, the more probable the individual is an abuser. At times, an abuser might have a couple of ways of behaving that the lady can perceive, yet they are very

misrepresented for instance, will attempt to make sense of the way of behaving as an indication of affection and concern; a lady might be complimented at

first. As times goes on, the ways of behaving become more serious and overwhelm and to control the woman.

1. Controlling behavior. At first the batterer will say this conduct is because of his anxiety for her wellbeing, her need to utilize her

time well, or her need to use sound judgment. He will lash out in the event that the lady is 'late' returning from the store or an arrangement; he will scrutinize her intently about where she went and with whom she talked. As the conduct advances, he

may not permit the lady to come to person conclusions about the house, kids, her attire, or going to chapel. He may

keep all the cash or even cause her to request authorization to take off from the house or room.

2. Jealousy. Toward the start of the relationship, the victimizer will say his desire is an indication of affection. Desire sits around aimlessly

with adoration. It is an indication of possessiveness and absence of trust.

The victimizer might scrutinize his accomplice about who she converses with, blame her for being a tease, engaging in extramarital relations, or being envious of the time she enjoys with family, companions, or youngsters. As the

envy advances, he might call her habitually during the day or drop by suddenly. He might decline to let her work for

dread she'll meet another person, or even start ways of behaving, for example, really looking at her vehicle mileage or requesting that companions watch her.

3. Quick involvement. Countless manhandled ladies dated or knew their victimizer for under a half year before they

were locked in, wedded, or living respectively. He comes in like a twister, guaranteeing, You're the one in particular who comprehends, or the one to focus on

I can converse with, the only one I've adored this much. He will constrain the lady to focus on the relationship so that the

lady might feel regretful or that she's letting him down' if she has any desire to dial back the inclusion or sever the relationship.

4. Unrealistic expectations. Abusive people will anticipate that their accomplice should address every one of their issues.

He anticipates an ideal spouse,

mother, darling, and companion. The abuser will make statements, for example, on the off chance that you love, I'm all you really want, and you're all I really want. The victimizer anticipates his accomplice to deal with everything for him genuinely and in the home.

5. Isolation. The abuser tries to cut his partner off from all resources and support.

If she has male friends, she's a whore.

If she has women friends, she's a lesbian.

If she's close to family, she's tied to apron strings. He accuses people who are her

support of causing problems. He may want to live in the country, without a phone, or refuse to let her drive the car, or he may

try to keep her from working or going to school.

6. Blames others for problems. Assuming he is persistently jobless, somebody is continuously treating him terribly or out to get

him. He may commit errors and afterward fault his accomplice for disturbing him and holding him back from focusing on the job that needs to be done. He might fault his accomplice for whatever turns out badly in his life.

7. Blames others for feelings. The abuser might tell his partner you make me distraught, you're harming me by not doing what I believe that you should do or then again, I can't resist the urge to be furious. He is the person who settles on the conclusion about what he thinks or feels, yet he will utilize these sentiments to control his partner.

8. Hypersensitivity. An abuser is effortlessly offended, asserting his sentiments are harmed, when in fact he is furious or taking the smallest mishap as an individual assault.

He will fly off the handle about the treachery of things that have occurred, things that are simply

a piece of living for instance, being approached to burn the midnight oil, getting a traffic ticket, or being told about irritating way of behaving.

9. Cruelty to children or animals. abusers might anticipate that kids should be fit for things past their capacities (rebuffs 18

month old for wetting diaper). He might prod kids until they cry. He may not believe youngsters should eat at the table or may anticipate them to be kept in their rooms when he is home. He might rebuff creatures mercilessly or be obtuse toward their aggravation or languishing.

10. Playful use of force in sex. An abuser might appreciate tossing the lady down or holding her down during sex. He might need to carry on dreams during sex where the lady is powerless. He is telling his accomplice that assault is invigorating. He may show little worry about whether the lady needs to have intercourse and utilizations scowling or outrage to maneuver her toward consistence. He might start having intercourse with the lady while she is resting or request sex when she is sick or tired.

11. Verbal abuse. As well as making statements that are deliberately intended to be horrible and frightful, obnoxious attack is likewise obvious in the abuser's debasing of his partner, reviling her, and deprecating her

achievements. The abuser tells her she is idiotic also, unfit to work without him.

The victimizer may likewise awaken her to loudly manhandle her or not let her nod off.

12. Rigid sex roles. The abuser anticipates that his partner should serve him. He might try and say the lady should remain at home and comply in all things-even demonstrations that are criminal in nature. The abuser considers ladies to be second rate compared to men, answerable for humble assignments, what's more, unfit to be an entire person without a relationship.

13.Dr. Jekyll/Mr. Hyde. The abuser keeps his partner befuddled by unexpected changes in his mind-set. She might accept he has some kind of mental issue since brief he's cherishing, and the following he's detonating. Touchiness and ill humor are

run of the mill of men who beat their partners.

14. Previous abusive relationships.

The abuser might say he has hit ladies before, yet fault them for the maltreatment they caused me to make it happen. His family members or ex-accomplices might caution her that he is oppressive. An abuser will mishandle any lady he is with if the

relationship endures long enough for the brutality to be presented.

15. Threats of violence. Threats of actual viciousness intended to control the accomplice: I'll kill you, I'll break your neck, and you would do well to be careful, or the

consequences will be severe. The vast majority don't compromise their partners; abusers will attempt to pardon their aggressive statements by saying, everyone talks like that.

16 Breaking or striking objects. Breaking valued belongings is utilized as discipline, however generally to threaten the lady

into accommodation. The abuser might beat on the table with his clench hand, or toss things around or close to his partner.

17 Any force during an argument. This might include the abuser keeping the lady from leaving a room, by limiting,

pushing, or pushing. He might hold his partner against the wall, telling her you will pay attention to me

CHAPTER THREE

Why Men Abuse Women And What Makes Them Stop

Courts must learn the basics about domestic violence Four decades after domestic violence first became a public issue, our courts still don't understand the causes and effective responses to domestic violence. Attempting to resolve DV cases without fundamental DV knowledge is like sending children to unregulated daycare; we keep seeing avoidable tragedies in which children are abused, and some die.

No research was accessible when aggressive behavior at home (DV) first turned into a public issue. Courts fostered their underlying reactions in view of well known presumptions that DV was brought about by substance misuse, psychological maladjustment, and the casualties' activities. This drove courts to go to emotional well-being experts for exhortation as though they were the specialists on abusive behavior at home.

In reasonableness, this misstep was made sincerely yet was never adjusted after research shown the underlying presumptions were off-base.

The Cause Of Domestic Violence Are Still Prevalent

The Women's Christian Temperance Movement advocated for prohibition at least partly because they believed excessive drinking caused husbands to viciously assault their wives. There was a logical basis for this assumption. Many men came home drunk and assaulted their wives. Alcohol does reduce inhibitions, so an abusive man under the influence would assault his wife more severely than if he was sober Accordingly, his drunken assaults were much more memorable.

We have since discovered that people don't participate in conduct they wouldn't consider when level-headed, regardless of whether they are affected by medications or liquor. Therefore, non-harmful men don't attack their partners regardless of whether they had an excessive amount to drink. The ones who attack their accomplices while impaired participate in an example of coercive and controlling way of behaving while sober and accept they reserve a privilege to control their accomplices. At the end of the day, substance misuse simply aggravates their maltreatment.

Additionally, most psychological maladjustments don't make men misuse their accomplices yet will make the attacks more extreme. Numerous men with different emotional well-being issues never misuse their accomplices. Dysfunctional behavior is a reason, yet it isn't the reason for abusive behavior at home.

people with outrage the board issues have no control over their indignation towards anybody. They are responsible to abuse their chief, a server, a bank employee, or a conveyance individual. Oppressive men just attack and misuse their accomplices and in some cases their kids. As such, their maltreatment depends on their male qualification and the conviction they have the honor to control their personal partners.

I frequently show the issue of outrage the board with an illustration of an abused and slighted by his chief. man.

He doesn't attack or obnoxiously assault his manager since he realizes there will be extreme outcomes. Still irate, he is halted for speeding returning from work. He doesn't think he merits a ticket however again controls his outrage since he realizes what occurs on the off chance that he goes after the cop. And afterward he returns home and attacks his partner.

The men in my batterer classes have recommended this is an unjustifiable model since they have no close to home connection to their chief or cop. Suppose they go from work to meet their accomplice at a party.

At the point when she accomplishes something he characterizes as inappropriate, he doesn't attack her at the party where there would be observers and outcomes. All things considered, he attacks her in the security of their home since he has valid justification to accept there will be no outcomes to him.

For each situation, the victimizer was completely fit for controlling his resentment in the event that it was for his potential benefit.

The law enforcement framework frequently involves mercy as a reaction to first-time wrongdoers. This can function admirably in different sorts of violations however is totally misled in DV cases. Aggressive behavior at home is the most underreported wrongdoing so whenever a abuser first comes to the consideration of the law enforcement framework is probably not going to be whenever he first perpetrated a wrongdoing, considerably less participated in other aggressive behavior at home strategies.

This might be the court framework's simply opportunity to change the elements.

Most victimizers let their casualties that know if they report their wrongdoings, nobody will trust them, or they have a workable method for keeping away from discipline. At the point when the court framework neglects to make a compelling move, it affirms all that he said. She faced a challenge in detailing his wrongdoing and might rebuffed for do as such. The court's inability to make significant results tells her they won't help her.

She won't ever tragically look for help from this point onward.

In any case, the law enforcement framework estimates its prosperity by rehash captures. Thus, the court accepts they made the best choice while the casualty experiences peacefully, and he can perceive guardianship courts and criminal courts he never mishandled anyone.

CHAPTER FOUR

Proven Response To Domestic Violence

In a real sense, billions of dollars have been spent attempting to demonstrate batterer programs are successful in forestalling aggressive behavior at home. The best outcome has been uncertain. One of the issues with a great deal of the examination is that men are not haphazardly doled out to batterer programs. Factors like the litigant's abundance, race, history of misuse, the seriousness of the wrongdoing, rehearses locally, connections of his lawyer, and expertise at control impact which abusers are relegated to batterer programs.

This implies there is no fair correlation with guilty parties relegated to a batterer program, different projects, or no results. The issue is additionally intensified by the way that DV is the most underreported wrongdoing, yet recidivism is the standard proportion of achievement.

The Middle for Court Development tried to manage the irregular testing issue by persuading decided in a review to relegate the guilty parties haphazardly to reactions like the batterer program, probation, or local area administration. The fundamental discoveries are that main responsibility and observing assist with changing victimizers' way of behaving. This finding is upheld by genuine models where networks that pre-owned rehearses in light of responsibility and checking saw a sensational decrease in abusive behavior at home wrongdoing, especially murders.

Ignorance Of DV 101 Has Consequences

The exploration is clear. Anyone can profit from treatment or from halting their substance misuse. People who truly have no control over their displeasure can profit from outrage the board programs. Batterer projects can furnish courts with unexpected ramifications for abusive behavior at home guilty parties.

Courts need to comprehend, in any case, that simply finishing any of these projects doesn't make an abuser safe. Regarding these projects as though it fixes the abusers jeopardizes his accomplice and the local area. Psychological maladjustment, substance misuse, and outrage issues separate from abusive behavior at home.

By the by, many courts treat these different issues as though they tackle the abusive behavior at home issue.

Batterer programs were made not in light of logical exploration but rather just on the grounds that it seemed like society required a reaction to aggressive behavior at home.

The issue is that it is a basic answer for a perplexing issue. In the Duluth Model, their batterer program should be a little piece of a lot more extensive local area reaction.

Men and young men get falsehood from many sources locally that energize the abuse of ladies. Our miserable history of enduring spouses' maltreatment of their wives upholds this falsehood. Networks should change crucial convictions, practices, and values to forestall abusive behavior at home.

Cities like Quincy, Nashville, and San Diego utilized a gathering of best practices that included severe implementation of criminal regulations, defensive orders, and probation rules; rehearses intended to make it simpler for casualties to leave; and composed local area reaction. These prescribed procedures prompted a sensational decrease in abusive behavior at home wrongdoing, particularly murder.

As of recently, our nation has been hesitant to roll out the improvements expected to forestall aggressive behavior at home all in all; they were reluctant to truly take aggressive behavior at home. Maybe the me too development; exposure around our careless authorization of assault and abusive behavior at home; and the recurrence that abusive behavior at home wrongdoers carry out mass killings will empower required changes.

The Expert (Unfriendly Youth Encounters) Exploration that shows youngsters presented to DV and other maltreatment will carry on with more limited and less sound lives ought to make public authorities rethink our careless reaction to abusive behavior at home. The US spends more than one trillion bucks every year to permit men to mishandle ladies. It resembles a secret duty that none of our lawmakers decided on. Maybe when this financial expense is better known, it will make the motivator required for the important changes.

Criminal courts need to force significant approvals for aggressive behavior at home and make discoveries so the victimizers can't later deny their violations. At the point when courts permit men to participate in treatment, outrage the executives, or substance misuse treatment as a substitute for responsibility, the courts discard a single opportunity to break the pattern of misuse.

Inappropriate tolerance is comparatively inadequate and upholds the message that society doesn't treat aggressive behavior at home in a serious way. These risky choices additionally show that the adjudicators and experts they depend on are new to the exploration each judge ought to have. It's a horrible idea to depend on ineffectual reactions when just responsibility and observing have been demonstrated to change abuses' way of behaving.

Not at all like crook courts, family courts are not intended to rebuff terrible way of behaving. It frequently feels like just moms attempting to safeguard their youngsters are rebuffed for doing what guardians should do. Judges seldom consider that rebuffing the mother is likewise rebuffing and hurting the children.

Authority courts depend on psychological well-being experts to answer abusive behavior at home reports. On the off chance that the victimizer likewise has a psychological well-being issue, he should get inadequate treatment and afterward be treated as protected. On the off chance that the victimizer breezes through his mental assessments, the courts accept he was unable to be a victimizer, and the mother should make bogus reports.

In one upstate New York authority case, the court perceived the dad's long history of misuse and restricted him to managed appearance. The people group doesn't have a directed appearance program, so the weight of finding fitting management was put on the person in question. The victimizer has been administered by companions and family members who frequently nod off or abandon him with the kids. Protests by the offspring of attacks and abuse during regulated visits have been accused on the mother.

The mother has been undermined with discipline when she can't find suitable bosses even after the dad's forceful conduct made it hard to keep managers. The overseer of a batterer program that doesn't depend on responsibility models guarantees the victimizer has changed. The court seems ignorant that it is untrustworthy for a batterer program to guarantee a victimizer is protected.

The reality a victimizer can act properly openly, as most victimizers do, enlightens us nothing concerning how he acts in private. Albeit the victimizer has kept on faulting the casualty for all that and gives off an impression of being following her and making bogus grumblings to youngster defensive administrations and others, the courts appear to consider regarding the abuser as though he is protected.

Court authorities liable for children wellbeing and security should comprehend that aggressive behavior at home isn't brought about by psychological sickness, substance misuse, outrage issues, or the casualty's activities. It is feasible for a victimizer to change, yet it seldom comes about pretty much by accident. It as a rule requires responsibility and checking. At the very least, a abuser changing his way of behaving would remember he is exclusively liable for the damage he has caused; he will be focused on never manhandling anybody from now on; and that's what will grasp assuming he at any point mishandles somebody, he will lose the relationship with his children.

Children really do benefit when they can have the two guardians in their lives.

They will be hurt in the event that they lose their relationship with their dad. The issue is that the damage of having a relationship with a victimizer is far more prominent than the mischief of having no relationship.

Pro lets us know that living with the trepidation and stress victimizers cause essentially abbreviates kids' lives and lead to a long period of wellbeing and social issues. It is a decision no adjudicator with information on Pro Exploration would make.

The main sensible arrangement is for the victimizer to change his way of behaving truly. Professing to change is only a continuation of his control.

Some Reasons Women Stay In Abusive Relationships

Numerous abusive behavior at home casualties don't shout out on the grounds that they dread being judged and compelled by others.

At the point when NFL linebacker Beam Rice thumped his life partner Janay Palmer oblivious in a lift in 2014, it didn't at first stand out enough to be noticed. He was blamed for aggressive behavior at home and suspended for two games. Following half a month, he was officially charged, yet he and Palmer were hitched the following day.

Nonetheless, when a security video of the occasion surfaced, it immediately became a web sensation. Watching Janay Palmer get wrecked and generally hauled out of the lift by Rice capably affected watchers.

The floods of shock that followed made the NFL scramble to expand their discipline of Beam Rice and direct an interior audit of their abusive behavior at home strategies.

Things took a fascinating turn when Janay Palmer stood up with regards to her significant other. She was sorry at a public interview saying. I profoundly lament the job I played that evening, and later requested that people stop their decisions and allegations. Simply realize we will keep on developing and show the world what genuine love is, she posted on Instagram, requesting that others not take a single thing from the man she cherishes.

This incited another public reaction.

Wary eyewitnesses couldn't comprehend how Palmer could be remaining by her man.

The assaults presently moved in the direction of her, with analysts scrutinizing her mental stability, blamelessness, and thought processes. How could somebody stay with, not to mention shield a man who had thumped her oblivious. What was off with Palmer that she would do this.

These accusations and questions prompted a pushback.

Casualties and ladies' promoters stood up with regards to Palmer and portrayed the confounded situations ladies in fierce connections face. Beverly Gooden, a HR chief in North Carolina, began a hashtag on

Twitter, why remained, where she shared her explanations behind leftover in a vicious marriage. I attempted to take off from the house once after an oppressive episode, and he hindered me, Gooden said, later adding.

I felt that affection would vanquish all. Her hashtag turned into a revitalizing point, with many casualties posting their accounts of the variables that kept them in oppressive connections.

As abusive behavior at home specialists, we were interested the way that these posts could assist experts and public eyewitnesses with bettering comprehend the one of a kind difficulties casualties of abusive behavior at home face. With partner Jaclyn Cravens, and doctoral understudy Rola Aamar,

I analyzed these voices to see what could be realized. We gathered many posts from ladies all around the world and read, coded, and arranged them, distributing these discoveries in 2015. Through this study, we recognized eight fundamental reasons women stay in abusive relationship:

1. Distorted Thoughts. Being controlled and harmed is damaging, and this prompts disarray, questions, and, surprisingly, self-fault. Culprits bug and blame casualties, which wears them out and causes depression and responsibility. For instance, ladies shared I accepted I merited it, and, I was embarrassed, humiliated, and accused myself since I assumed I set off him. Others limited the maltreatment as a method for adapting to it, saying I remained in light of the

fact that I didn't believe that profound and monetary maltreatment was truly misuse. Since words don't leave wounds, and, in light of the fact that I didn't have the foggiest idea how my beau treated me was assault.

2. Damaged Self-Worth. Related was the harm to the self that is the consequence of debasing treatment. Numerous ladies felt whipped and of no worth, saying He caused me to accept I was useless and alone, and, I believed I misunderstood followed through with something and I merited it.

3. Fear. The danger of real and close to home mischief is strong, and abusers utilize this to control and keep ladies trapped. Female survivors of viciousness are substantially more reasonable than male casualties to be threatened and damaged.

One said I feared him I realized he'd make leaving a revolting somewhat long bad dream. Endeavoring to leave an abuser is hazardous. One lady felt caught in light of her significant other's intentions to chase me down and hurting all my friends and family including our children while I watched and afterward killing me.

4. Wanting to be a Savior. Many depicted a craving to help, or love their accomplices with the expectations that they could transform them I accepted I could cherish the maltreatment out of him. Others portrayed inside values or responsibilities to the marriage or accomplice, with tweets like: I figured I would be areas of strength for the who might never leave him and show him unwaveringness. I would fix him and show

him love. Others had pity and put their accomplice's necessities over their own:

His dad passed on, he turned into a drunkard and said that God wouldn't believe I should leave him since he wanted me to improve him.

5 Children. These ladies likewise put their youngsters first, forfeiting their own wellbeing I was apprehensive on the off chance that he wasn't beating me, he would beat his children. Furthermore, I esteemed their lives more than my own. What's more, I remained for quite some time while I safeguarded our youngsters, all while I was being manhandled. Others referenced remaining to help the youngsters I believed that my child should have a dad.

6. Family Expectations and Experiences. Many posted portrayals of how previous encounters with viciousness mutilated their identity or of sound connections: I watched my father beat my mother. Then I found somebody very much like father, or, on the grounds that raised by creatures, you collaborate with wolves. Some referenced family and strict tensions My mom let me know God would abandon me assuming I broke my marriage.

7 Financial Constraints. Many alluded to monetary restrictions, and these were frequently associated with really focusing on kids I had no family, two small kids, no cash, and responsibility since he had mind harm from a fender bender. Others couldn't keep occupations on account of the abusers

control or their wounds, and others were utilized monetarily by their victimizer My ex piled up a huge number of unpaid liabilities in my name.

8. Isolation. A typical strategy of manipulative accomplices is to isolate their casualty from loved ones. Some of the time this is physical, as one lady experienced, I was in a real sense caught in the boondocks of WV, and he would utilize my son to keep me close. Different times disconnection is personal, as one lady was informed You can either have loved ones or you can have me.

Albeit these eight purposes behind remaining are normal, they don't depict each casualty and circumstance. Ladies can likewise be culprits, and there are many examples of brutality. However, these posts give convincing insider's perspectives on the challenges of going with choices in a savage relationship, and this is useful for untouchables to comprehend. One explanation numerous casualty wonder whether or not to shout out is on the grounds that they fear being judged and constrained by companions and experts. On the off chance that more people answered casualties' accounts of maltreatment with concern and sympathy, rather than with analysis, more casualties could shout out and find the help they need to carry on with a daily existence liberated from misuse.

CHAPTER FIVE

Why Domestic Abuse Happens

Whether alcohol and drug use are a factor or not, domestic violence and abuse is a very serious problem for the victims and the abusers. Although studies seem to indicate some link between alcohol/drug misuse and domestic violence, others believe that they are two separate issues.

Domestic abuse is not so much about a loss of control as it is about total control. Ironically, many batterers do not see themselves as perpetrators, but as victims. This reasoning is common among batterers and many have elaborate denial systems designed to justify or excuse their actions.

About Control

There are shifting hypotheses about what compels batterers misuse those nearest to them. One view is that batterers are solidified hoodlums who perpetrate their wrongdoings in a cognizant, determined way to accomplish the strength they accept they are qualified for. Others accept misuse is the result of profound mental and formative scars.

Specialists have arrived at an agreement on a few normal qualities among batterers.

Accept that men have a pre-appointed right to be responsible for all parts of a relationship.

Mate Retention Behaviors

For certain abusers, savagery is a device to hold their close accomplice back from leaving the relationship or holding them back from being untrustworthy, regardless of whether it implies genuinely constraining them to remain.

One investigation discovered that much of the time, demonstrations of abusive behavior at home are mate maintenance ways of behaving that is, moves initiated by one accomplice to attempt to save and keep up with their relationship with the other partner.

As one batterer made sense of in the wake of going through treatment, the maltreatment was about control: I could cause her to do anything I desired. I was attempting to scare her. I needed to control her for the basic explanation that I realized I could make it happen. It caused me to feel strong, he proposed.

The Warning Signs Of Domestic Abuse

The issues of power and control are essential to an understanding of domestic violence. One way this is accomplished is by becoming familiar with the cycle of violence. Here is an overview of the phases.

Develop Stage: The strain constructs

Stand-Over Stage: Obnoxious ambushes increment

Blast Stage: A savage eruption happens

Regret Stage: The victimizer pardons their way of behaving (You shouldn't have pushed me, it was your issue.)

Pursuit Stage: Commitments are made (It won't ever occur from now on, I guarantee.)

Vacation Stage: A short relief before the cycle starts once more.

Different Types of Misuse

This cycle concerns genuine actual maltreatment. It doesn't consider different types of homegrown maltreatment that are utilized to control, for example,

Monetary maltreatment

Mental and psychological mistreatment

Sexual maltreatment

Social maltreatment

Profound maltreatment

Obnoxious attack

Relationship Misuse Is Brought About By

Relationship misuse is a decision and it is a scholarly way of behaving.

Therefore, it is hard to say that relationship misuse is brought about by any one single variable. Nonetheless, the accompanying convictions and perspectives are normal for victimizers:

Relationship Abuse Is Caused By

Relationship abuse is a choice and it is a learned behavior.

For these reasons, it is difficult to say that relationship abuse is caused by any one single factor. However, the following beliefs and attitudes are common for abusers.

Social Forces

Social forces also play a pivotal role in shaping an abuser's values and attitudes, as well as creating an environment where abusive behavior is rewarded and unpunished. The following social forces may contribute to perpetrators' decision to abuse:

Gender-role identity Limited definitions of appropriate masculine behavior that glorify aggression, violence, and dominance.

Family Messages that men should have the power and make decisions in a household and/or intimate relationship (e.g. a man's home is his castle)

Media Portrayals of women as objects; glorification of violence and violent, coerced, and non-consensual sex; limited male and female roles.

Peer group social pressure to conform to a limited definition of masculinity, which centers on devaluing women.

Sports Competition, aggression, and dominance are praised. Teammates that demonstrate sexist and/or abusive behavior are not held accountable.

Impunity Many perpetrators do not face any negative repercussions for their sexist attitudes and abusive behaviors. If they are challenged, their excuses are accepted e.g. blaming the behavior on alcohol use, stress, or being provoked by the victim.

Relationship Abuse Is NOT Caused By

Research has shown that relationship abuse is NOT caused by the following factors:

Provocation

Behavior of victim or problems in the relationship

Stress

Drugs or alcohol

Testosterone

Genetic factors

Loss of control or Anger

Communication problems

Illness or mental health issues

Culture

Poverty

Many people experience these factors and do not abuse.

These are excuses perpetrators will use to justify their behavior.

If the perpetrator is trying to blame their behavior on something else other than their own choice, they are not holding themselves accountable.

Theories Of Violence

Throughout history, societies around the world have systematically devalued and oppressed women. In the US, moves toward make close accomplice misuse unlawful started exclusively in the 20th 100 years. Many keep on considering men's viciousness against ladies to be a verifiable issue, yet actually 1 out of 3 ladies overall and in the US keep on being mishandled and assaulted by an accomplice. It was only after 1993 that conjugal assault was viewed as a wrongdoing in each of the 50 states. Having a typical comprehension of the reasons for abusive behavior at home can assist networks with growing more powerful reactions to casualties and culprits. Such a comprehension assists us with abstaining from offering clashing reactions that could subvert endeavors to safeguard casualties and consider batterers responsible.

Feminist Theory

Women's activist hypothesis sees men's brutality against ladies because of a man centric design. Male centric method for control is frequently inconspicuous and profoundly dug in, with the most incredibly vicious structures holding off on arising until male centric control is compromised as when individual ladies leave or take steps to leave connections or gatherings of ladies declare their freedoms.

Gelles (1997)) Intimate Violence in Families

The women's activist orientation governmental issues model hypothesis about aggressive behavior at home holds that male command over ladies is available in numerous areas, going from close connections to financial life. Most men don't mishandle women, however any man can be a culprit. Furthermore, any lady can turn into a casualty: there has been no particular character quality found that makes a person bound to encounter misuse the essential common quality of casualties is being female. Survivors of relationship misuse are frequently compelled to remain in those connections due to fear, absence of help, and casualty accusing by companions and bigger networks.

Trade or decision hypothesis expands on the women's activist model, recommending that men decide to act harmfully toward their female accomplices since they can pull off it and on the grounds that doing so gets them what they need as power and control. At last, men misuse ladies since they can.

Survivor hypothesis grasps ladies' conduct in harmful connections as the advancement of ways of dealing with hardship or stress. Her absence of choices and assets make leaving troublesome, and when she looks for help, she frequently observes it to be deficient. Bombed endeavors to leave or get help end in her getting back to the abusers, and manhandle may heighten.

Historical Theories Of Violence

The accompanying speculations were generally proposed to make sense of and figure out orientation savagery. These are not generally viewed as exact in the field.

Codependency hypothesis recommended that survivors of misuse became reliant upon their abusers. This viewpoint on orientation brutality neglects to perceive the power differential among people and wrongly pathologizes casualties of viciousness.

Social learning hypothesis expressed those men became harmful in light of the fact that they had learned brutality in their families, while ladies searched out oppressive men since they saw their moms being mishandled. Be that as it may, numerous offspring of oppressive men and siblings of vicious men don't manhandle, and ladies who saw maltreatment in youth are not any more liable to be mishandled than ladies who didn't. In light of how normal maltreatment is, it is feasible for one lady to encounter maltreatment from more than one source during her lifetime, yet this doesn't imply that she is searching out misuse. Eventually, the oppressive accomplice is the person who decides to viciously act. Learned defenselessness hypothesis recommended that casualties of misuse stay in harmful connections in light of the fact that delayed maltreatment strips them of their will to leave. In all actuality, manhandled ladies constantly make a move to safeguard themselves, and frequently ladies are compelled to conclude that remaining out of the blue is many times her most secure choice, in light of the great counter rate.

Pattern of brutality hypothesis, expresses those oppressive connections by and large comprise of three stages: a pressure building stage, where the harmful accomplice becomes crabby, controlling, and possibly obnoxiously harmful while the lady treads lightly; a dangerous stage, where viciousness is available; and a vacation stage, in which the harmful accomplice wins back the lady with blossoms and conciliatory sentiments. This is obsolete on the grounds that it isn't predictable with ladies' encounters. Numerous ladies report that there was no continuous development of strain, but instead inconsistent, unusual episodes of savagery. Moreover, others never experience a vacation stage. At the point when they do, this is all the more precisely depicted as the control stage, since it is a control strategy with respect to the abuser.

Frameworks hypothesis considers maltreatment to be just a consequence of brokenness inside the relationship.

This model proposes that the two accomplices add to the heightening of outrage. Bograd (1984) contends that the frameworks hypothesis approach is frequently perilous in light of the fact that it overlooks the power lopsidedness in relationship misuse and it suggests that the survivor is somehow or another answerable for the maltreatment. It is normal for couples to lash out or baffled with one another, however turning out to be obnoxiously or truly oppressive is dependably a decision. Frameworks hypothesis might be applied for normal issues in a relationship, however ought not be used in instances of relationship misuse.

www.ingramcontent.com/pod-product-compliance
Lightning Source LLC
LaVergne TN
LVHW052050160826
845678LV00015B/3150

* 9 7 9 8 8 4 8 7 5 2 2 4 3 *